RESOURCE BANK

ADDITION AND SUBTRACTION FACTS

CONTENTS

INTRODUCTION	1
ACES TO TENS	
USING 1 TO 10	4
FACTS TO 20	8
DOUBLES AND TREBLES	12
H, T AND U	
ADDING TO TENS	16
LOTS OF TENS	24
TENS AND HUNDREDS	28
DOUBLING HUNDREDS	32

About this book

Addition and subtraction facts presents a structured collection of maths activities, built around the use of an A1 poster which displays two sets of numbered playing cards (1–10) on one side and plain cards numbered in hundreds, tens and ones on the other.

The book is divided into seven sections which form a developmental sequence. It provides work ranging in level from Reception/Primary 1 to Year 3/Primary 4. Each section contains interactive whole-class activities, games and group activities, as well as photocopiable activity sheets to help the children practise skills. Ideas for differentiation and extension work are included, as well as relevant suggestions for classroom display. An indication is given of the intended age range or ability level for each activity, in line with the National Numeracy Project.

About number facts

The skills of adding numbers together and subtracting numbers from other numbers form the basis of arithmetical calculation. When children have experience of counting objects and combining small sets of objects to find the total, the next step is to introduce them to the skill of representing the sets of objects with numbers and adding these numbers together. Initially, children will continue to use objects or mathematical apparatus to help them. When they understand the principles and are sufficiently familiar with the processes, the next step is to encourage them to carry out calculations mentally.

Number facts are sets of arithmetical statements. In the context of early work on arithmetic, they are commonly associated with children knowing, for example, that certain pairs of numbers when added together make 10; or that when one of a pair of

INTRODUCTION

numbers is subtracted from 10, the other number is left. It is hoped that knowledge of such 'facts' will enable children to carry out subsequent calculations involving these pairs of numbers mentally.

The base 10 number system

The structure of the base 10 number system, counting up from ones (units) to tens, then hundreds, thousands and so on, provides a logical basis for children to develop an understanding of the numbers in this system. It enables children to start by working with small numbers up to 10, then build up gradually to working with much larger numbers, while developing their skills in carrying out calculations and solving arithmetical problems.

At each stage, children require plenty of practice in handling numbers. They need to work not only with objects, apparatus and/or pencil and paper, but also with the numbers themselves, in order to develop their mental arithmetic skills. This can be achieved through activities which help them to learn key number facts, the place value relationships between numbers and the use of mental strategies such as doubling and trebling numbers.

All the activities in this book are carefully designed to help children develop mental arithmetic skills by developing their knowledge of important number facts, including an understanding of the relationships between ones, tens and hundreds and the use of doubling and trebling strategies. Some of the activities may appear to be similar in nature. This continuity is intended to help children recognize the connections between work they have covered and new work they are carrying out. For example, the activities include games and written tasks that involve using numbers to 10. This is then extended to cover numbers to 20, then to 100 and finally to 1000, using further number games and written tasks supported by the sets of cards from the poster.

Many of the games are designed so that they can be played at any spare moment, to keep children's skills sharp. Most of the photocopiable sheets are designed as open-ended tasks, so that they can also be used for activities that are not described in this book.

Playing cards and numbered cards

The playing cards and plain numbered cards on the poster can provide the basis for a wide range of whole-class and group activities. Playing cards have the advantage of providing children with objects (shapes) to count as well as numbers. Numbered cards have the advantage of offering a counting frame which can be used flexibly according to the children's stage of development. A class or group could work with the sets of cards 1–5, 1–10 and 1–20; with cards numbered in ones, tens or hundreds; or with a combination of ones, tens and hundreds.

In contrast to the 'fixed sums' on paper, children can make their own 'sums' with the cards and then move cards around to group easy addition pairs together. Cards can also provide a basis for many number games and investigations, such as the magic square puzzles in this book (see page 14).

NB It is important that children only attempt to work with playing cards or numbered cards that display numbers within their personal counting frame (that is, numbers to which they can count confidently, and which they can recognize in written form).

The National Numeracy Framework for Teaching

National concern about poor standards of numeracy has led to recommendations that more emphasis be placed on whole-class interactive teaching and the application of mental arithmetic skills in solving everyday problems.

Work with playing cards and numbered cards lends itself readily to teacher-directed whole-class and small-group mental arithmetic activities and games. Whole-class and group work, number games and individual

INTRODUCTION

pencil-and-paper practice all help children to sharpen their understanding of key number facts and relationships between numbers, and to develop confidence in applying their mental skills in everyday situations where arithmetical calculations are required.

The activities in this book are designed to support the development of mental arithmetic skills and early addition and subtraction strategies, as set out for children in the age range R–Y3 in the National Numeracy *Framework for Teaching*. They are equally appropriate for teachers of young children following the Scottish National Guidelines for Mathematics 5–14 or the Northern Ireland Curriculum for Mathematics.

Preparing to use the poster

The A1 coloured poster in this book displays two sets of playing cards: aces (1s) to 10s in diamonds and clubs. Pages 4–15 contain activities, designed to support class work at different stages of development, which use this poster as a focus.

The A1 black and white poster on the reverse side displays cards numbered in hundreds (100–1000), tens (10–100) and ones or units (1–10). Pages 16–32 contain activities which use this poster as a focus.

Whichever side is being used, the poster should be displayed where it is clearly visible to the class and accessible to those who wish to look more closely. It can be used as a wall-mounted teaching chart for whole-class work or mounted on a portable easel for small-group work. It can also be laid flat on a table or the floor as a focus for interactive group work. Many of the activities in this book also include the use of a flip chart, chalkboard or large sheet of paper for building patterns of number facts, demonstrating ways of working and recording children's ideas.

Both sides of the poster can usefully be supported with matching cards. Sets of numbered or plain cards are available from educational suppliers. Alternatively, you could photocopy the black and white poster several times onto thin card, then cut out and laminate the resulting cards. The cards can be modified to suit the age and ability of your class – enlarging and colour-coding them may be appropriate.

Other uses of the poster

Each set of playing cards on the coloured poster could be cut out, mounted on card and laminated for use with a set of matching playing cards or coloured counters as a matching activity for younger children.

Either side of the poster could also be used as the centrepiece for a wall display of children's work on number facts.

LET'S LOOK AT THE POSTER

GROUP SIZE AND ORGANIZATION
Whole class, working with the teacher on the carpet.
DURATION
10–15 minutes.
LEARNING OBJECTIVE
To become familiar with the numbers on the playing cards poster through a number matching activity.

YOU WILL NEED
The playing cards poster; a shuffled set of playing cards 1–10 in diamonds and clubs. (You may need to combine the cards from two packs to provide enough cards for each child.)

WHAT TO DO
Pointing to each of the diamond cards on the poster in turn; ask the children to say the numbers, so that they count aloud to 10. Then point randomly to various diamond cards and ask individual children to say the number on the card. Do the same with the club cards.

Give out one playing card to each child. Tell the children that you are going to point to a card on the poster; if they have that card, they must hold it up and say what it is (for example, 'Nine of clubs'). If the ace cards you are using have an 'A', explain that this stands for 'Ace' but counts as '1' – so the child should say, for example, 'One of clubs'. Play the game, pointing to the cards on the poster in a random order.

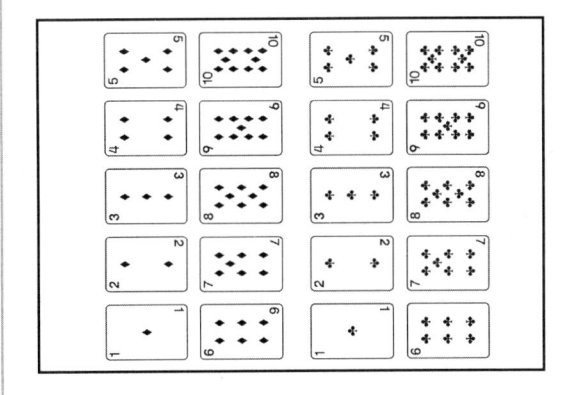

ADDITION AND SUBTRACTION FACTS   RESOURCE BANK

ACES TO TENS
USING 1 TO 10

MAKING 10

GROUP SIZE AND ORGANIZATION
Whole class, working with the teacher on the carpet (R/P1–Y1/P2).
DURATION
10–15 minutes.
LEARNING OBJECTIVE
To develop recall of the number facts of 10.

YOU WILL NEED
The playing cards poster, a set of playing cards 1–10 of diamonds, a flip chart and marker pen (or chalkboard and chalk).

WHAT TO DO
Tell the children that they are going to work with only the red cards (the diamonds) on the poster; when you hold up a card, they have to find the number that goes with it to make ten. Start by holding up the ace of diamonds and asking: *What number goes with 1 to make 10?* Choose a child to point to the appropriate card on the poster. Write the corresponding sum on the flip chart: 1 + 9 = 10. Now hold up the 2 of diamonds, and so on. Repeat the process in reverse order, starting with 10.

When the children are familiar with the principle, shuffle the cards and hold them up in a random order, asking children to say the sum – for example, '3 and 7 make 10'. Tell them to look at the flip chart if they need help. Finally, remove the 'workings' on the flip chart from view and hold up the cards in a random order to check that the children can find the pairs unprompted.

ASSESSMENT
Note whether the children can say and point to the correct numbers on the poster when the cards are held up in ascending or descending order. Note whether they can work out the correct numbers to make 10 mentally, or whether they need to look at the 'workings' on the chart.

IDEAS FOR DIFFERENTIATION
With younger children, you could carry out the same activity using playing cards numbered 1–5 and the first line of cards on the poster. Ask the children to find numbers to make 5. This can be increased to 6, 7 and so on, gradually building up to 10.

With older children, you could extend the activity by holding up a card and asking the children to subtract the number from 10. Go through the cards in ascending and then descending order before shuffling them and holding them up in random order.

IDEAS FOR DISPLAY
A chart showing the addition facts of (or 'number stories about') 10 can be made up for display in the classroom.

'QUICK 10S' GAME

GROUP SIZE AND ORGANIZATION
A group of 4 children, working with the teacher (R/Y1).
DURATION
20–30 minutes.
LEARNING OBJECTIVE
To practise building the addition facts of 10 and recording the sums.

YOU WILL NEED
A set of shuffled playing cards (1–10 of diamonds) and a set of 10 cubes for each group; a sheet of plain or squared paper and a pencil for each child; a flip chart and marker pen (or chalkboard and chalk).

WHAT TO DO
NB The children should carry out and be familiar with the previous activity, 'Making 10', before playing this game.

Explain to the children that they will each be given one playing card, face down, at the start of the game.

ACES TO TENS
USING 1 TO 10

When you say 'Ready, steady, go!', they should turn over the card, write its number on their sheet and then complete an addition sum to make 10. Use the flip chart to demonstrate – for example, turning over a 3 and writing '3 + 7 = 10'. The children may use their cubes to help them if necessary. When they have completed writing the sum, they should give the card back and receive another card. The first child to write 10 sums is the winner. (If they are given a card they have already used, they should ask for another card.)

Play the game a few times, so that the children can increase their speed and improve their recall of the number facts.

ASSESSMENT
Check whether the children can complete the sums by recalling the number facts, or whether they need to use cubes (or their fingers).

IDEAS FOR DIFFERENTIATION
Additional support can be provided for less able children by displaying a chart showing the addition facts of 10.

With younger children, a 'Quick 5s' game could be played using the diamond playing cards 1–5 and sets of five cubes. The first child to complete five sums is the winner. Go on to 'Quick 6s', and so on.

With older children, the game could be changed to 'Subtract from 10': the children have to subtract the number on the card from 10 and record their answer each time (for example, 10 – 4 = 6).

'PAIRS TO MAKE 10' GAME

GROUP SIZE AND ORGANIZATION
4 children at a table or on the floor, working with the teacher (Y1/P2–Y2/P3).
DURATION
20–30 minutes.
LEARNING OBJECTIVE
To practise finding pairs of numbers that add up to 10.

YOU WILL NEED
Two sets of nine playing cards (1–9 of diamonds), a flip chart or chalkboard showing all the addition pairs that make 10 (see 'Ideas for display' in 'Making 10', page 4), a marker pen or chalk.

WHAT TO DO
NB The children should have some knowledge of the addition complements of 10 in order to play this game.

Shuffle the cards and spread them face down on the table or floor. Tell the children that they have to find two cards that add up to 10. The players take turns to turn over a pair of cards. If the cards add up to 10, the child keeps them and takes another turn. If the cards do not add up to 10, they are turned face down again and the next child takes a turn. The player with the most pairs at the end wins. Tell the children they can look at the chart if they need help.

ASSESSMENT
Note whether the children are sufficiently familiar with the addition complements of 10 to play the game mentally, or whether they need to look at the chart.

IDEAS FOR DIFFERENTIATION
For younger children, addition pairs making 6 can be written on the flip chart; the game can be played with two children and two sets of diamond cards numbered 1–5, the players trying to find pairs of numbers that add up to 6.

The 'Pairs to make 10' game can be made easier for less able children by allowing them to start by picking up one card and laying it face up in front of them. (If two children pick up the same number card, the child who picked it up first keeps it and the second child picks up another card.) Ask each child in turn to say what number he or she needs to make 10. They should then take turns to turn over one card at a time,

ADDITION AND SUBTRACTION FACTS

ACES TO TENS
USING 1 TO 10

turning each 'wrong' card face down again, until they find the card with the number they need – then pick up another card, lay it face up and so on.

For older children, the game can be made more complex and demanding by using more than one suit of cards showing the numbers 1–9 (for example, using both diamonds and clubs). When the children are very familiar with the game, all four suits of cards numbered 1–9 can be used.

ADDING TWO NUMBERS

GROUP SIZE AND ORGANIZATION
Children working individually in small groups (Y1/P2–Y2/P3).
DURATION
40 minutes.
LEARNING OBJECTIVE
To carry out addition with pairs of numbers between 1 and 10.

YOU WILL NEED
Photocopiable page 7, pencils.

WHAT TO DO
NB The children need to be able to count and write numbers to 20 in order to do this activity.

Give each child a copy of photocopiable page 7. Explain to the children that they have to complete this sheet by adding together the numbers on each pair of cards joined by arrows, then writing the answers in the boxes. When the children have completed their sheets, discuss the number patterns (going up in 2s) in each line of 'answer' numbers. (See Figure 1.) Ask: *Are there any pairs of numbers that give the same answer?* (For example, 3 and 4, 1 and 6; 4 and 9, 6 and 7.)

ASSESSMENT
Note whether the children can add the pairs of numbers in their heads, or whether they need to count the diamonds on the cards. Note whether they can describe the number patterns made by the answer numbers, and identify pairs of numbers that give the same answer.

EXTENSION WORK
The children can use another copy of page 7 to find the difference between the numbers on each each pair of cards joined by arrows. When they have completed the sheet, discuss the number patterns in each line of 'answer' numbers. (See Figure 2.)

IDEAS FOR DISPLAY
The children can each be given a small piece of white card and a number between 1 and 10 to make their own diamond playing cards, using red crayons or felt-tipped pens. The completed photocopiable sheets and cards can be mounted to create a display of work on addition.

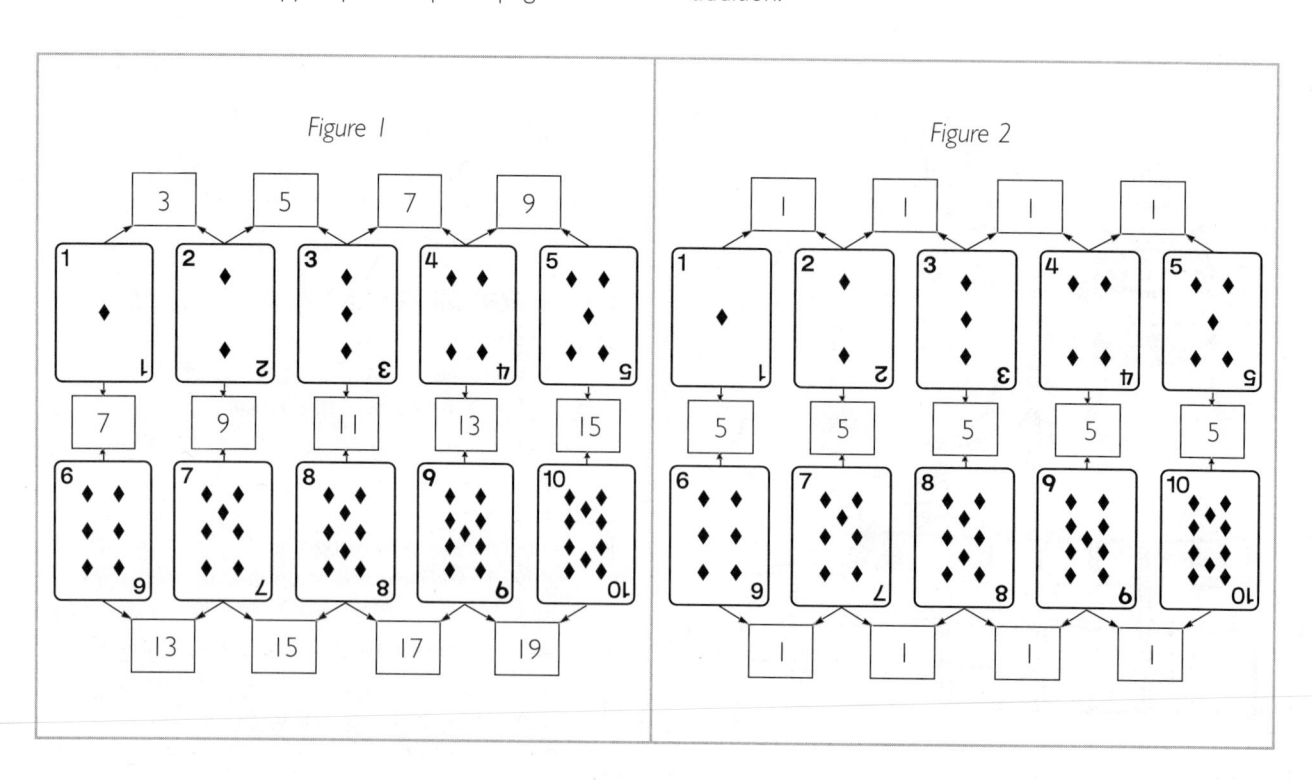

Figure 1

Figure 2

ACES TO TENS
USING 1 TO 10

Name _____ Date _____

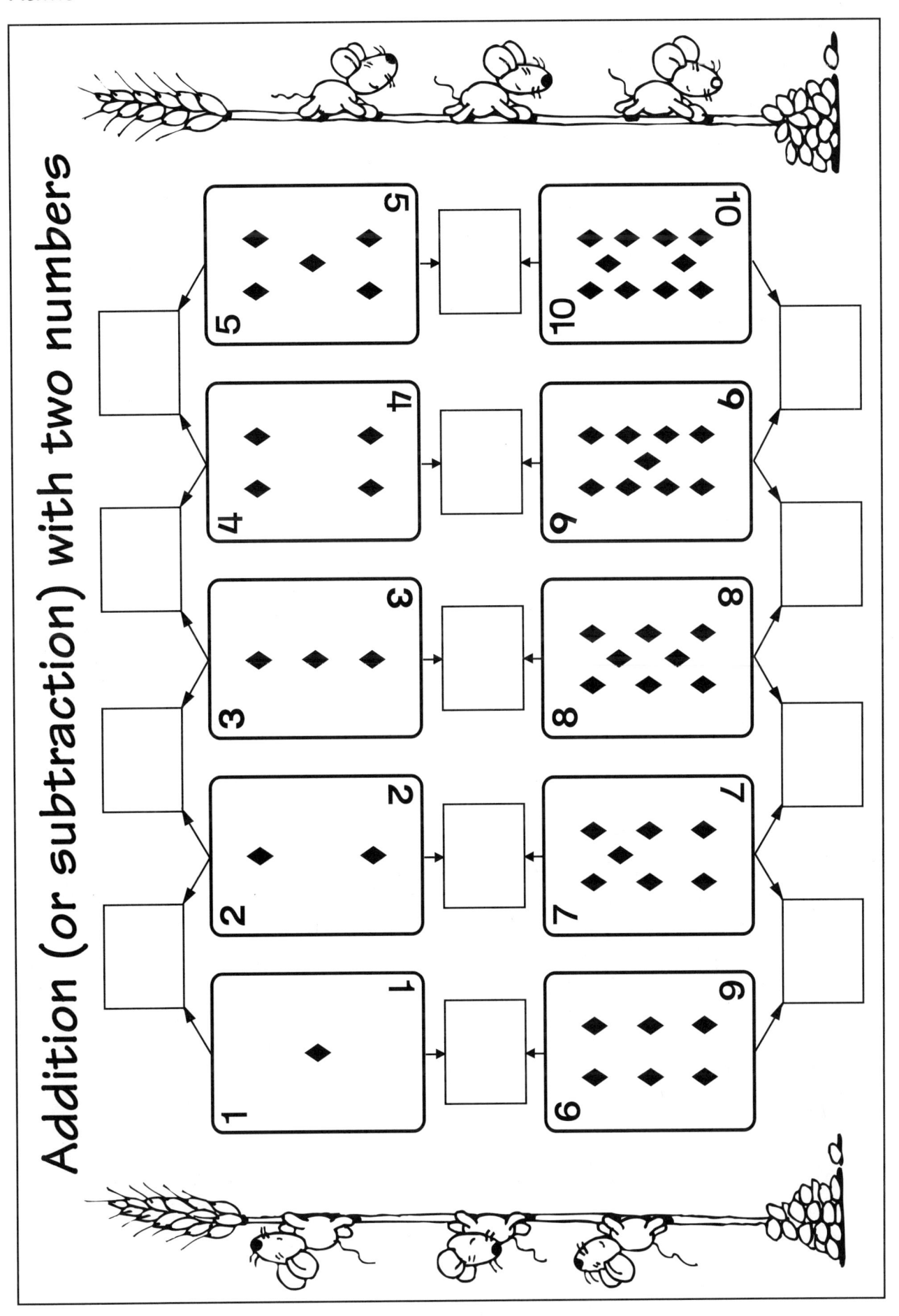

Addition (or subtraction) with two numbers

ACES TO TENS
FACTS TO 20

10 PLUS

GROUP SIZE AND ORGANIZATION
Whole class, seated on the carpet (Y1/P2–Y2/P3).
DURATION
10–15 minutes.
LEARNING OBJECTIVE
To become familiar with adding numbers on to 10 to make the numbers from 10 to 20.

YOU WILL NEED
A flip chart and marker pen (or chalkboard and chalk), the playing cards poster.

WHAT TO DO
Use the flip chart to build up the pattern of adding numbers to 10:

10 + 1 = 11
10 + 2 = 12 ... and so on.

Choose a child to give the answer each time, and invite him or her to write it on the chart.

Explain to the children that you are going to point to a card on the poster and they will have to add the number to 10 and give the answer – for example, by saying '10 add 7 makes 17'. Point to a different card on the poster each time, choosing a different child to give the answer.

As the children become familiar with this game, play it without referring to the poster or the flip chart: simply call out a number and ask a child to give the answer (for example, you say '8' and the child says '18').

ASSESSMENT
Note whether the children can add the numbers mentally, or whether they need to look at the flip chart to find the answer.

EXTENSION WORK
Build up a similar pattern of subtracting numbers from 20 on the flip chart:

20 – 1 = 19
20 – 2 = 18 ... and so on.

Play the game as above, asking the children to subtract the number on the card from 20 each time and state the answer – for example, '20 take away 7 makes 13'.

ADDING TWO NUMBERS

GROUP SIZE AND ORGANIZATION
A group of 4–6 children, working individually (Y1/P2–Y2/P3).
DURATION
40 minutes.
LEARNING OBJECTIVE
To practise adding two numbers between 1 and 10 in order to make the numbers from 10 to 20.

YOU WILL NEED
The playing cards poster (laid flat on the table or displayed on the wall), photocopiable page 10, pencils, a flip chart and marker pen (or chalkboard and chalk).

WHAT TO DO
Use the flip chart to make a large copy of the first diagram on page 10. Ask the children to look at the poster and tell you two numbers that will add up to 11. Write a suggested pair of numbers as a sum in the empty box on the diagram. Can they find another two numbers? Invite a child to write another sum under yours on the board; continue until no more pairs of numbers can be found. (See Figure 3.) If a child suggests a reversed pair (for example, 8 + 3 after 3 + 8), accept this, but discuss the underlying principle (that $a + b = b + a$) with the children.

Give each child a copy of photocopiable page 10. Tell the children that they have to find as many different pairs of numbers as they can to make each number on the sheet, writing the pairs of numbers as sums in the correct boxes. They can do this by choosing one diamond card and one club card from the poster, counting the shapes on the cards or adding the numbers together in their heads; then they can write that pair of numbers in the correct box on the sheet.

Figure 3

11
10 + 1
9 + 2
8 + 3
7 + 4
6 + 5

RESOURCE BANK

ADDITION AND SUBTRACTION FACTS

ACES TO TENS
FACTS TO 20

ASSESSMENT
Note whether the children can add the numbers together mentally, or whether they have to count up the diamonds and clubs on the cards.

IDEAS FOR DIFFERENTIATION
For younger children, use separate playing cards. Working with a group of four children, lay out the diamond cards 1–5 and the club cards 1–5 in the middle of the table (as in Figure 4). Give each child a sheet of plain or squared paper and a pencil. Tell them that they have to look at the cards and choose two (one of each suit); then write out a sum using the two numbers, add them together and write down the answer. To help the children remember which cards they have chosen, they can each be given two cubes of the same colour (a different colour for each child) to place on the cards.

Older children could be asked (when they have completed the sheet) to find different ways of making 15 with **more than** two cards, and to record their answers on the back of their photocopied sheet.

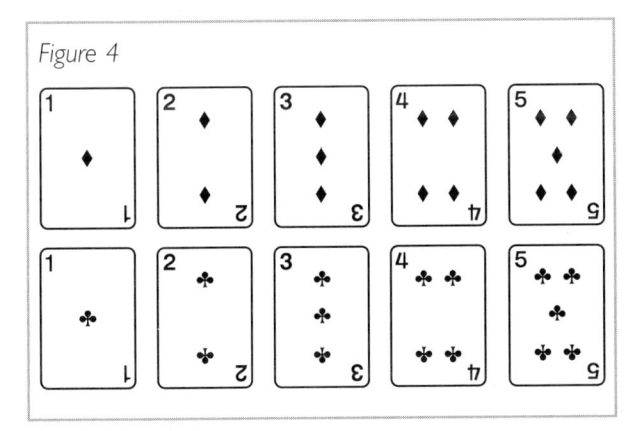

Figure 4

MAKING 20

GROUP SIZE AND ORGANIZATION
A small group, working individually with the teacher (Y1/R2–Y2/R3).
DURATION
20–30 minutes.
LEARNING OBJECTIVE
To find different ways of making 20 by adding three numbers.

YOU WILL NEED
The playing cards poster (laid flat on a table or displayed on the wall), photocopiable page 11, pencils, a flip chart and marker pen (or chalkboard and chalk).

WHAT TO DO
Use the flip chart to make a large copy of one of the triangle diagrams on page 11. Ask the children to look at the poster and find three numbers which add up to 20. They should raise their hands when they have found the numbers. Invite a child to write his or her numbers in the corners of the diagram on the flip chart. Check with the rest of the group whether these numbers add up to 20. Do this a few times, because some of the numbers chosen initially may give the wrong total.

When the children have demonstrated that they understand the task, remove the 'workings' on the board from view and give out copies of photocopiable page 11 for the children to complete. They should start by writing the rule 'Making 20 with three numbers' at the top of the sheet, then find ten different sets of three numbers.

Encourage them to add the easiest pair of numbers first and then add on the third number. Tell them that double numbers can be included. Point to relevant cards on the poster to help the children see what to do – for example, use diamond cards 4 and 6 to give 10, then use club card 10 to make 20.

ASSESSMENT
Note whether the children can add the numbers together mentally, or whether they need to count the diamonds and clubs on the cards (or use their fingers). Note whether they add the numbers together in a random order or look for the easiest pair first. Note those children who work systematically through a set of solutions.

IDEAS FOR DIFFERENTIATION
More able children could be encouraged to make 15 using three numbers, and to use subtraction in some solutions – for example, 9 + 8 – 2 (see Figure 5). Alternatively, they could look for ways to make 20 using four cards, recording their solutions on a copy of photocopiable page 23.

EXTENSION WORK
The children could go on to 'grow' a 20 plant, a 25 plant or a 30 plant with six numbers, using photocopiable page 30 (see 'Grow a 200 plant', page 28).

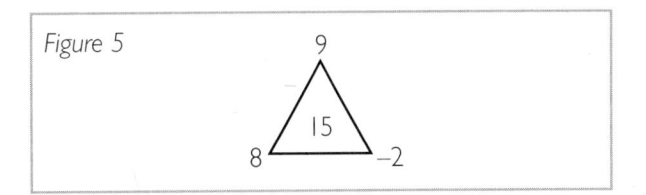

Figure 5

ADDITION AND SUBTRACTION FACTS   RESOURCE BANK

ACES TO TENS
FACTS TO 20

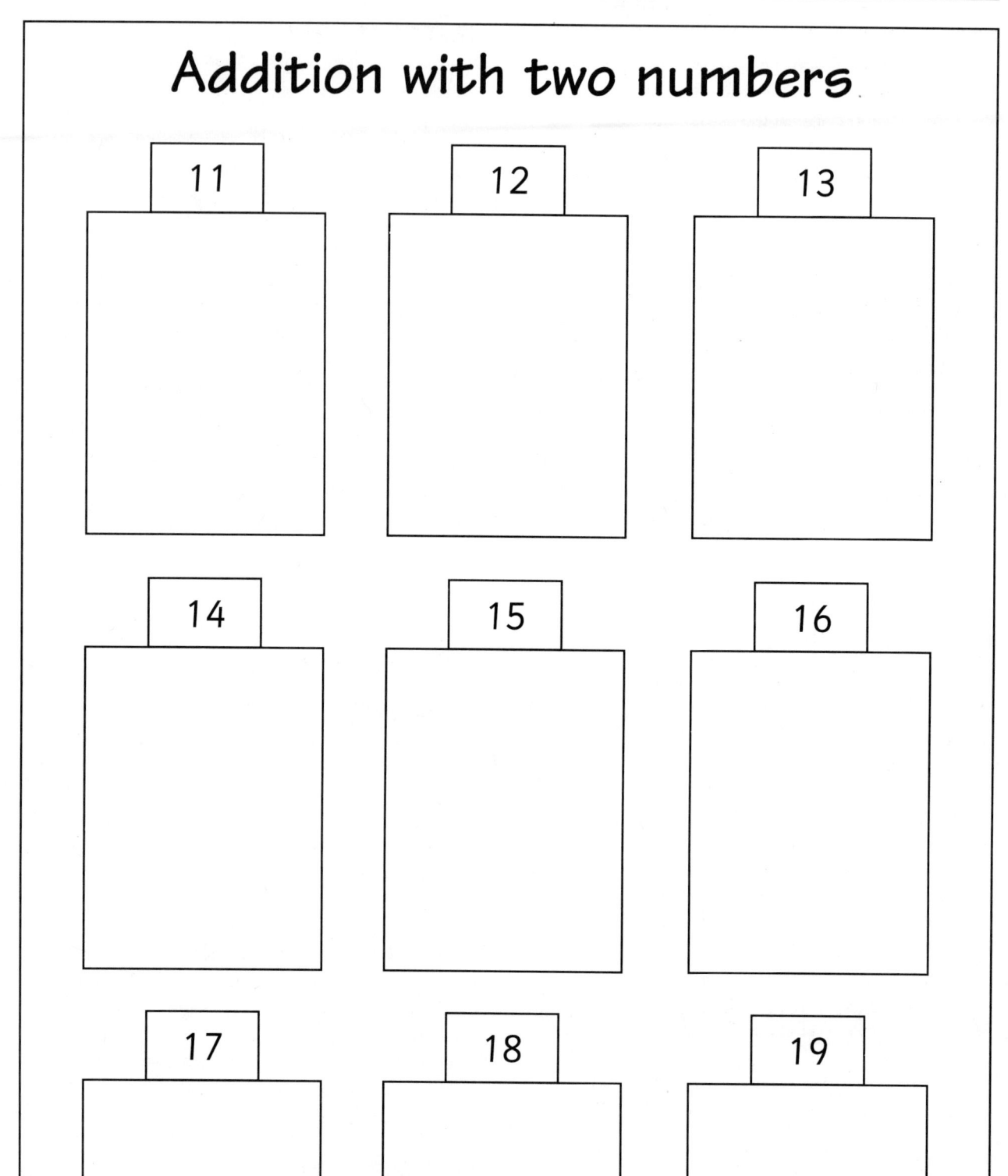

Name _____ Date _____

Addition with two numbers

11	12	13
14	15	16
17	18	19

ADDITION AND SUBTRACTION

ACES TO TENS
FACTS TO 20

Name _____ Date _____

Rule:

ADDITION AND SUBTRACTION

ACES TO TENS
DOUBLES AND TREBLES

QUICK DOUBLES

GROUP SIZE AND ORGANIZATION
Whole class on the carpet (Y1/P2–Y2/P3).
DURATION
10–15 minutes.
LEARNING OBJECTIVE
To develop the skill of doubling numbers (by addition).

YOU WILL NEED
The playing cards poster, a flip chart and marker pen (or chalkboard and chalk), a set of shuffled playing cards (diamonds and clubs 1–10).

WHAT TO DO
Point to the two aces on the playing cards poster and write the sum 1 + 1 = on the flip chart. Ask a child to say the answer ('Double 1 is 2') and to write it on the flip chart. Then point to the two 2s and write the sum 2 + 2 = on the board. Ask the children whether they know what comes next. Use the flip chart to build the pattern of double numbers from 1 to 10.

Next, use the set of shuffled playing cards. Hold up one card at a time and ask a child to say what the double of the number is – for example, 'Double 4 is 8.' Allow the children to refer to the flip chart, but encourage them to give quick responses based on mental calculation.

Conclude the activity by removing the poster and flip chart from view and playing the 'Quick doubles' game again.

ASSESSMENT
Note whether the children can double numbers mentally, or whether they need to look at the flip chart or the poster (counting the diamonds and clubs) or use their fingers.

EXTENSION WORK
Build the pattern of treble numbers on the flip chart:
1 + 1 + 1 =
2 + 2 + 2 = ... and so on.

Ask a child to say the answer and write it on the board each time; then ask the children to tell you what comes next.

Use the playing cards to play the game 'Quick trebles', in which the child chosen has to triple the card number shown (saying, for example, 'Treble 4 is 12').

BEAT THE TEACHER

GROUP SIZE AND ORGANIZATION
A group of 4 children, seated at a table or on the floor with the teacher (Y1/P2–Y2/P3).
DURATION
20–30 minutes.
LEARNING OBJECTIVE
To reinforce mental doubling skills.

YOU WILL NEED
The playing cards 1–10 in all four suits.

WHAT TO DO
Spread out the cards face down on the table or floor. Ask the children to take turns in turning over two cards. When they have found two cards showing the same number, they have to say the double number (for example, 'Double 3 is 6'). If they get the answer right, they keep the pair; if they get it wrong, the teacher takes the pair. If two cards are turned over that are not doubles, they are turned face down again and the next child takes a turn. When there are no cards left on the table, the player with the most cards wins.

ASSESSMENT
Note whether the children can double the numbers mentally, or whether they need to count the shapes on the cards.

IDEAS FOR DIFFERENTIATION
For younger children, use only the playing cards numbered 1–5; as they develop their mental doubling skills, introduce cards showing 6, then 7 and so on to the game.

For less able children, reduce the number of cards on the table by using only two suits of cards (diamonds and clubs) with the numbers 1–10. For older children, make the game more challenging by using two packs of playing cards to make two sets of cards numbered 6–10 in all four suits.

ACES TO TENS
DOUBLES AND TREBLES

HUNT THE TREBLE

GROUP SIZE AND ORGANIZATION
A group of 4 children, seated at a table or on the floor (Y1/P2–Y3/P4).
DURATION
20–30 minutes.
LEARNING OBJECTIVE
To develop the skill of trebling numbers (by addition).

YOU WILL NEED
Playing cards numbered 1–10 in diamonds, clubs and hearts.

WHAT TO DO
NB The children should have some experience of calculating treble numbers before carrying out this activity. (See the extension activity for 'Quick doubles' on page 12.)

Spread out the cards face down on the table or the floor. The game starts with each child picking up one card and laying it face up in front of him or her. If two children pick up the same number card, the child who picked it up first keeps it and the second child replaces the card and picks up another. The children then take turns to turn over one card at a time, looking for another card with the same number. If the card does not match their first card, they have to turn it face down again. When they find a matching card, they can pick it up and lay it next to the first card.

When they have found two cards that match their first card, they call out 'Treble!' and say the total (for example, 'Treble 3 is 9'). If they get the total right, they keep the three cards and take another starting card. If they get it wrong, the three matching cards are given to the teacher. When no cards are left on the table, the player with the most cards is the winner.

ASSESSMENT
Note whether the children can treble the numbers mentally, or whether they need to count the shapes on the cards.

IDEAS FOR DIFFERENTIATION
For younger children, use two packs of playing cards to make two sets of cards numbered 1–5 in diamonds, clubs and hearts.

For older children, make the game more challenging: use two packs of playing cards to make two sets of cards numbered 6–10 in diamonds, clubs and hearts.

'BUILDING TREBLES' GAME

GROUP SIZE AND ORGANIZATION
Children working in small groups with the teacher (Y1/P2–Y3/P4).
DURATION
20–30 minutes.
LEARNING OBJECTIVE
To practise trebling numbers (by addition) and recording the totals.

YOU WILL NEED
Photocopiable page 11, pencils, at least one pack of playing cards.

WHAT TO DO
NB The children should have some experience of calculating treble numbers before carrying out this activity. (See the extension activity for 'Quick doubles' on page 12.)

Give each child a copy of photocopiable page 11 and a pencil. Give each group one suit of shuffled playing cards numbered 1–10 (diamonds for one group, clubs for another and so on). Tell the children that the game starts with each child being dealt one card. When you say 'Ready steady go!' they must write their number in the three squares on the first diagram on the sheet, then write the total in the centre. Figure 6 (overleaf) shows an example.

When they have done that, they should give the card back and receive another card. If they have already used the number on the new card, they must take another card. The first child to find 10 trebles is the winner. If there is time, give out more copies of the sheet and play the game again.

ASSESSMENT
Note whether the children are able to find the treble numbers mentally, or whether they need to count the shapes on the cards (or use their fingers) to find the totals.

IDEAS FOR DIFFERENTIATION
For younger children, use only cards numbered 1–5 (this will mean that they have to use each card twice to complete the sheet).

For less able children, provide a box of number rods or interlocking cubes to help them build the treble numbers.

ADDITION AND SUBTRACTION FACTS — RESOURCE BANK

ACES TO TENS
DOUBLES AND TREBLES

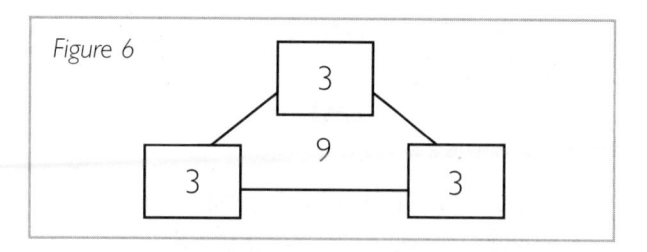

Figure 6

[Figure 6: Triangle arrangement with 3 at top, 3 at bottom-left, 3 at bottom-right, and 9 in the middle]

MAGIC SQUARE PUZZLE

GROUP SIZE AND ORGANIZATION
A group of 6–8 children, working in pairs with the teacher (Y2/P3–Y3/P4).
DURATION
20–30 minutes.
LEARNING OBJECTIVE
To practise addition using three sets of treble numbers.

YOU WILL NEED
Photocopiable page 15, squared paper, pencils, a flip chart and marker pens (or chalkboard and chalk).

WHAT TO DO
Give each pair a copy of photocopiable page 15, a sheet of squared paper and a pencil. Use the flip chart to display a large nine-square grid with numbers written in a line underneath, as in Figure 7. Tell the children that they have to put each number in a square on the grid so that all the horizontal, vertical and diagonal lines add up to 6.

They can draw as many nine-square grids as they like on the squared paper to try out their ideas. When they have got it right, they should copy the correct version onto the photocopiable sheet, writing '6' in the 'magic number' box. Figure 8 shows a correct solution. Four other solutions are possible – all with a diagonal line of 2s.

NB It is important for you to direct this activity, as some children may need some guidance in getting started – for example, you might suggest: 'Start with the diagonal lines.'

ASSESSMENT
Note whether the children are able to tell you about the 'special' feature of the magic square: all the 2s are in a diagonal line. Check whether they can reproduce the square correctly from memory on the back of the photocopiable sheet.

IDEAS FOR DIFFERENTIATION
For younger children, provide each pair with a set of nine numbered cards instead of the squared paper, so that they can rearrange the cards until they find a correct solution.

For older children, when they have completed the first square, give them another copy of page 15 and ask them to make a magic square with three 2s, three 3s and three 4s such that all the lines add up to 9. When they have done this, encourage them to compare their square with the first one: *What do you notice about how the numbers in both squares are arranged?* (All the 3s are in a diagonal line.) If there is time, they can be invited to make a square from three 3s, three 4s and three 5s:
◆ *Can you predict what the 'magic number' will be?* (12)
◆ *What about 4s, 5s and 6s?* (15)
◆ *Can you say what the rule is for making these magic squares?* (All the 'middle' numbers are in a diagonal on the square. The 'magic number' is treble the middle number.)
◆ *Can you make a magic square with higher numbers and find the magic number?*

IDEAS FOR DISPLAY
The completed photocopiable sheets can be mounted and made into a wall display of magic squares, or incorporated into a display of work with number facts. For a centrepiece, each child can draw and colour in a large picture of a playing card on a sheet of paper or card to match one of the numbers used: 1s, 2s and 3s in three different suits. These can be mounted to form a magic square, with the completed sheets arranged around it. All the children can draw and colour in smaller versions of different playing cards on paper; these can be attached to strips of paper and placed around the edge to form an attractive border.

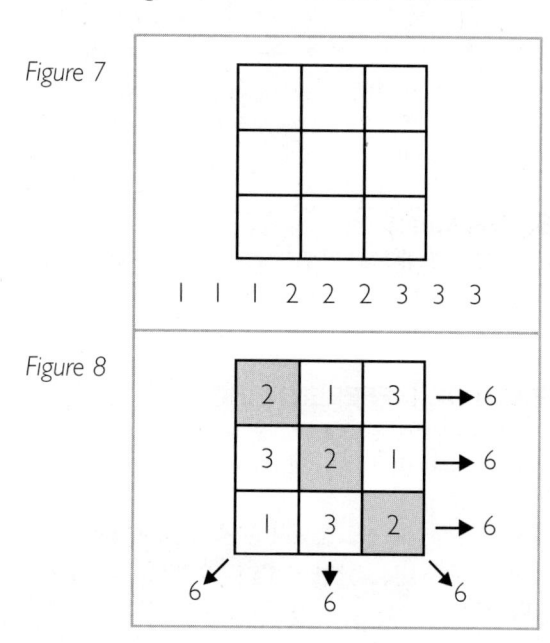

Figure 7

[Figure 7: Empty 3×3 grid with numbers "1 1 1 2 2 2 3 3 3" listed below]

Figure 8

[Figure 8: 3×3 magic square:
Row 1: 2, 1, 3 → 6
Row 2: 3, 2, 1 → 6
Row 3: 1, 3, 2 → 6
Columns and diagonal all equal 6]

ADDITION AND SUBTRACTION

ACES TO TENS
DOUBLES AND TREBLES

Name —————————— Date ——————————

Magic square puzzle

The magic number is: ☐

H, T AND U
ADDING TO TENS

TENS AND UNITS

GROUP SIZE AND ORGANIZATION
Whole class on the carpet (Y2/P3–Y3/P4).
DURATION
10–15 minutes.
LEARNING OBJECTIVE
To add units to tens mentally.

YOU WILL NEED
The hundreds, tens and units poster.

WHAT TO DO
Start by asking all the children to count aloud in 1s to 100. Then point to a tens number on the poster (for example, 20) and ask a child to count from that number to the next ten in 1s (in this case, from 20 to 30). Repeat the process for several other tens numbers. If a child gets stuck, invite all the class to join in for that count.

Seat the children in a circle to play a 'Quick addition' game. Point to a tens number on the poster, then a units number, and say (for example) 'Vicky, 20 add 4?' or 'Ranjit, 40 add 2?' Ask each child in turn.

ASSESSMENT
Note whether the children can add the numbers mentally or whether they need to use their fingers.

EXTENSION WORK
Ask all the children to count backwards in 1s from 100. Then point to a tens number on the poster and ask a child to count backwards from that number to the next tens number in ones. Repeat for several tens numbers, inviting the class to join in if a child gets stuck. Play a 'Quick subtraction' circle game in the same way as the 'Quick addition' game: the child chosen has to subtract the ones number from the tens – for example, 'Joanna, 30 take away 3?'
NB This extension is much more difficult than the main activity. For children who are less confident with counting backwards from 100 and subtracting from numbers above 10, it will be useful to introduce the idea by pegging the numbers 1–10 (drawn on pieces of paper or card) on a washing line in front of the class to help the children subtract different 'ones' numbers. When the children appear confident with the activity, display the numbers 10–20 on the line and repeat; then display the numbers 20–30, and so on.

TENS AND UNITS (2)

GROUP SIZE AND ORGANIZATION
A group of 4 children, seated at a table with the teacher (Y2/P3–Y3/P4).
DURATION
20–30 minutes.
LEARNING OBJECTIVE
To practise adding tens and units numbers and recording the totals.

YOU WILL NEED
A sheet of plain or squared paper, a pencil and an empty box (or rectangular margarine tub) for each child; four sets of cards numbered 1–10 and four sets of cards numbered 10–90 in tens (these could be made from photocopies of the black and white poster); some interlocking cubes or counters. **Tip:** Mark the backs of each set of cards with a different coloured shape, so that the sets can be sorted out easily after each game. Fasten each set with an elastic band after the activity, ready for future use.

WHAT TO DO
Give each child a set of tens cards and a set of units cards, shuffled and placed face down in two piles in front of them. Tell them that when you say 'Ready, steady, go!' they should take one card from the top of each pile, add the two cards together and write the sum on the sheet of paper (for example, 20 + 6 = 26). Then they should put the two cards into their box and take two more cards. The first child to finish is the winner.

After the game, check that the children have written the sums correctly. Ask each child to sort out the cards in the box into two piles, shuffle the cards and then play the game again. The game can be played several times, with a cube (or counter) given to the winner of each round. Only award a cube if all the sums are correct. At the end of the session, the cubes can be counted up to find the overall winner.

ASSESSMENT
Note whether the children are able to add the numbers together mentally or whether they need to count on their fingers. Note whether they record the sums correctly.

IDEAS FOR DIFFERENTIATION
For younger or less able children, set the 'tens' number at a single value (such as 20) and give them only a

H, T AND U
ADDING TO TENS

shuffled pile of 'ones' cards. The children can turn over one card at a time, add it to 20 and write the sum on the paper. Children who are less confident with subtraction could also be given individual copies of a 0–99 number square to help them with this activity.

For older children, set up the game as in the main activity, but ask them to subtract the 'ones' card from the 'tens' card and record the number sentence (for example, 30 – 7 = 23) each time.

ADDING THROUGH TENS

GROUP SIZE AND ORGANIZATION
A group of four children (of similar ability) working with the teacher (Y2/P3–Y3/P4).
DURATION
20–30 minutes.
LEARNING OBJECTIVE
To carry out addition through tens with units numbers.

YOU WILL NEED
A flip chart and marker pen (or chalkboard and chalk). For each child: at least two copies of photocopiable page 20, a pencil, a set of shuffled cards numbered 5–60 in 5s, four small boxes or margarine tubs. Have some small 0–99 number squares available for children who need help.

WHAT TO DO
Draw a large copy of the circle diagram from page 20 on the flip chart. Ask the children to count aloud in 5s. Tell them that you are going to write the numbers counting in 5s in the boxes around the circle. Write 5 in the first box and ask *What number will be in the next box?* Write 10 in the next box, and so on. Give the children a copy each of photocopiable page 20 and ask them to write the numbers counting in 5s around the circle, using the flip chart to help them. Now ask them to write the rule 'Add 6' inside the circle. Figure 9 shows how their sheets should look now.

Start the game by giving each child a shuffled set of numbered cards (in a pile face down in front of them) and a tub or box. They have to take a card from the pile, add 6 to the number and write the answer in the correct circle on the sheet. They can then put the card in the tub and take another card. The first child to run out of cards is the winner.

Play the game again, using the rule 'Add 7'. If there is time (or in a later session), use the rules 'Add 8' and 'Add 9'.

ASSESSMENT
Note which numbers the children are able to add mentally, and which numbers they add using a number square or their fingers.

IDEAS FOR DIFFERENTIATION
For younger children, prepare some copies of the sheet with the numbers counting in 5s around the circle already written in. Ask them to add 6 to each number, going round in order; then give them another sheet and ask them to add 7 to each number. Children who need help could also be given a 0–99 number square to refer to.

For older children, prepare some copies of the sheet with the numbers counting in 5s around the circle from 15 to 70. Change the rule of the game with cards to 'Subtract 6', then 'Subtract 7', and so on. (See Figure 10.)

For practice work with addition or subtraction through tens, a range of different sheets can be made from page 20 by filling in the boxes with a different set of numbers (counting in 5s) each time. Figure 11 shows an example.

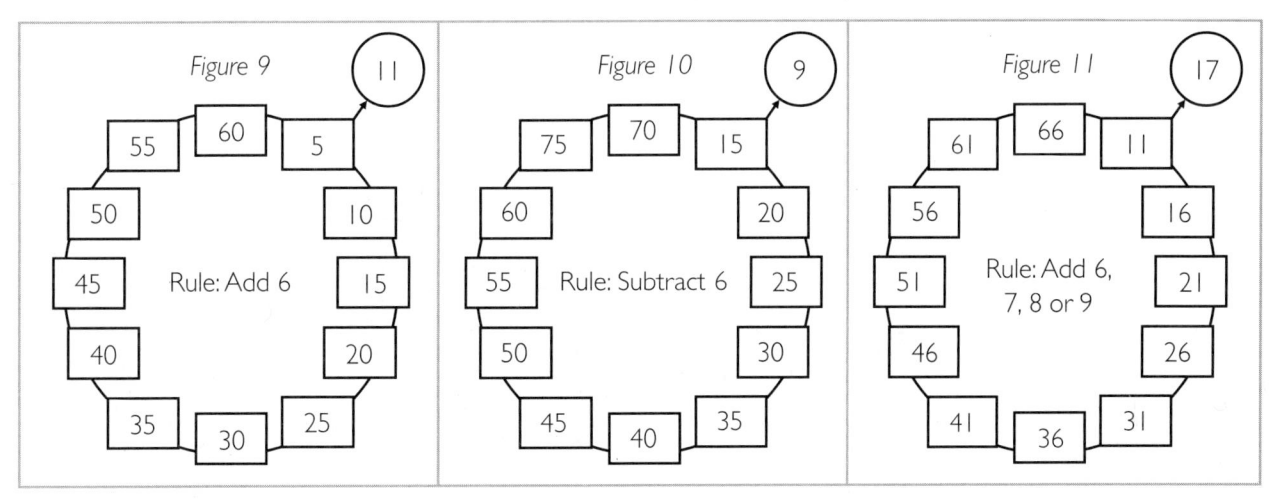

Figure 9 — Rule: Add 6 (circle with 5, 10, 15, 20, 25, 30, 35, 40, 45, 50, 55, 60; answer 11)

Figure 10 — Rule: Subtract 6 (circle with 15, 20, 25, 30, 35, 40, 45, 50, 55, 60, 70, 75; answer 9)

Figure 11 — Rule: Add 6, 7, 8 or 9 (circle with 11, 16, 21, 26, 31, 36, 41, 46, 51, 56, 61, 66; answer 17)

ADDITION AND SUBTRACTION FACTS

H, T AND U
ADDING TO TENS

Figure 12

| 3 | 5 | 6 | 8 | 30 | 40 | 50 | 60 | 80 |

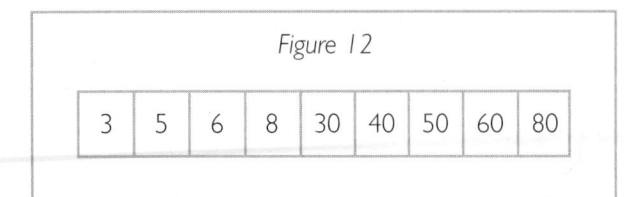

FOUR IN A LINE GAME

GROUP SIZE AND ORGANIZATION
Pairs of children working at a table or on the floor, with a child or adult as referee (Y2/P3–Y3/P4).
DURATION
20–30 minutes.
LEARNING OBJECTIVE
To carry out addition with tens numbers and units numbers.

YOU WILL NEED
For each pair: a copy of photocopiable page 21; two sets of counters or cubes (a different colour for each child); a set of cards numbered 3, 5, 6, 8, 30, 40, 50, 60 and 80. If a child is the referee, provide a calculator. Have a set of Cuisenaire rods available for any child who needs help.

WHAT TO DO
Lay out the numbered cards in a line on the table or floor, face up (see Figure 12). Tell the children that they must take turns to choose any two cards, pick them up and lay them in front of them. They must then add them together to make a number in one of the circles on the board (page 21). The referee checks the answer. If it is correct, the player covers the number on the board with a counter and replaces the cards in the line; if it is wrong, the player just replaces the cards and play passes to the other child.

The winner is the first player to get four of his or her counters in a straight line (horizontal, vertical or diagonal). Figure 13 shows some examples of lines which can be made on this board.

NB As this game involves the use of strategy, photocopiable page 21 should be mounted on card and laminated for use at other times. Until the children are familiar with the rules, it is better if an adult acts as referee.

ASSESSMENT
Note whether the children can add the numbers mentally, or whether they need to use rods or fingers. Are they selecting numbers on the basis of strategies to make lines or block their opponents' lines, or are they simply selecting numbers because the addition is easy?

IDEAS FOR DIFFERENTIATION
Differentiation will arise through repeated playing, as the children become familiar with adding the numbers and develop strategies for placing the counters on the board.

IT ALL ADDS UP

GROUP SIZE AND ORGANIZATION
Children working individually in small groups (Y2/P3–Y3/P4).
DURATION
20–30 minutes.
LEARNING OBJECTIVE
To carry out addition with two tens numbers and one units number, recording the totals.

YOU WILL NEED
The hundreds, tens and units poster; photocopiable page 22, pencils. Provide some Cuisenaire rods or interlocking cubes for children who are less confident with addition of tens and units.

WHAT TO DO
Using the hundreds, tens and units poster and a copy of photocopiable page 22, explain to the children that

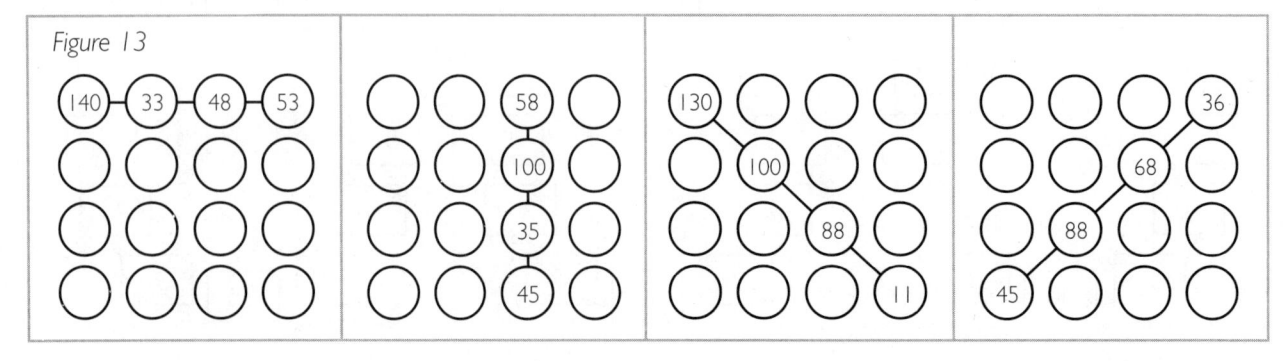

Figure 13

H, T AND U
ADDING TO TENS

they have to select two tens numbers and one units number from those on the sheet, add them together and then write the answer as a sum (starting with the tens number) on the sheet. For example: 20 + 10 + 3 = 33. They should fill in the 'rule' box with 'Addition of tens and units.'

Encourage the children to add the tens together first and then count on the units. They should make as many different sums as possible.

ASSESSMENT
Note whether the children can add the numbers mentally, or whether they need to use structural apparatus. Note whether they can record the sums correctly.

IDEAS FOR DIFFERENTIATION
Younger children could start by placing a counter on each of the three numbers they have chosen and writing down the sum; then they could use Cuisenaire rods to represent the numbers and find the total, adding the tens together first and then counting on the units.

Older children could be encouraged to try some numbers where the total will be more than 100.

IT ALL ADDS UP (2)

GROUP SIZE AND ORGANIZATION
Small groups, the teacher working with individuals (Y2/P3–Y3/P4).
DURATION
40 minutes.
LEARNING OBJECTIVE
To carry out addition with two tens numbers and two units numbers.

YOU WILL NEED
The hundreds, tens and units poster; photocopiable page 23, pencils. Provide some counters and Cuisenaire rods or interlocking cubes for children who are less confident with addition of tens and units, and calculators for the children to check their answers (if appropriate).

WHAT TO DO
Using the hundreds, tens and units poster and a copy of photocopiable page 23, explain to the children that they have to choose two different 'tens' numbers and two different 'ones' numbers from those on the poster,

then write them in the four circles on the first diagram on the sheet. They should then add the numbers together and write the answer in the middle of the diagram. They should fill in the 'rule' box with 'Addition of tens and units.' They should then repeat the process with different numbers.

Encourage the children to add the 'tens' numbers together first, then add the 'ones' numbers together and then find the total. They may wish to write the 'tens' and 'ones' sub-totals as 'workings' on the sheet to help them (see Figure 14).

When they have completed their sheets, ask the children to exchange sheets with a partner and check each other's answers, or to check their own answers, with a calculator.

ASSESSMENT
Note whether the children are able to find the totals mentally, or whether they need to write down some 'workings' to help them. If they cannot find any of the totals mentally, can they represent the numbers with Cuisenaire rods, group the tens and units together and count on to find the total?

IDEAS FOR DIFFERENTIATION
Younger children could work with a copy of photocopiable page 22 instead of page 23. Tell them to choose four numbers on the sheet and place a counter on each, then write down the sum starting with the tens numbers (for example, 40 + 10 + 5 + 2). Encourage them to work out the answer mentally. If they need help, ask them to represent the numbers with Cuisenaire rods and find the total by adding the tens together and then counting on the units. Let them check their answers with a calculator.

Older children could be encouraged to choose numbers where the total will be more than 100.

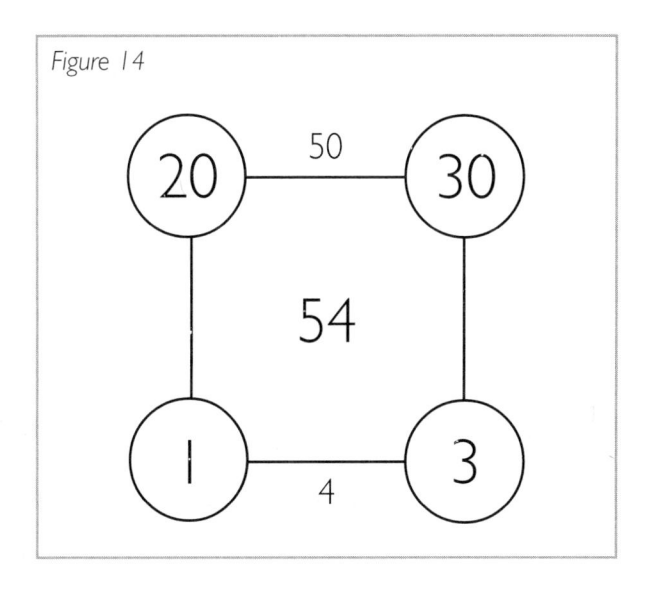

Figure 14

H, T AND U
ADDING TO TENS

Name _____ Date _____

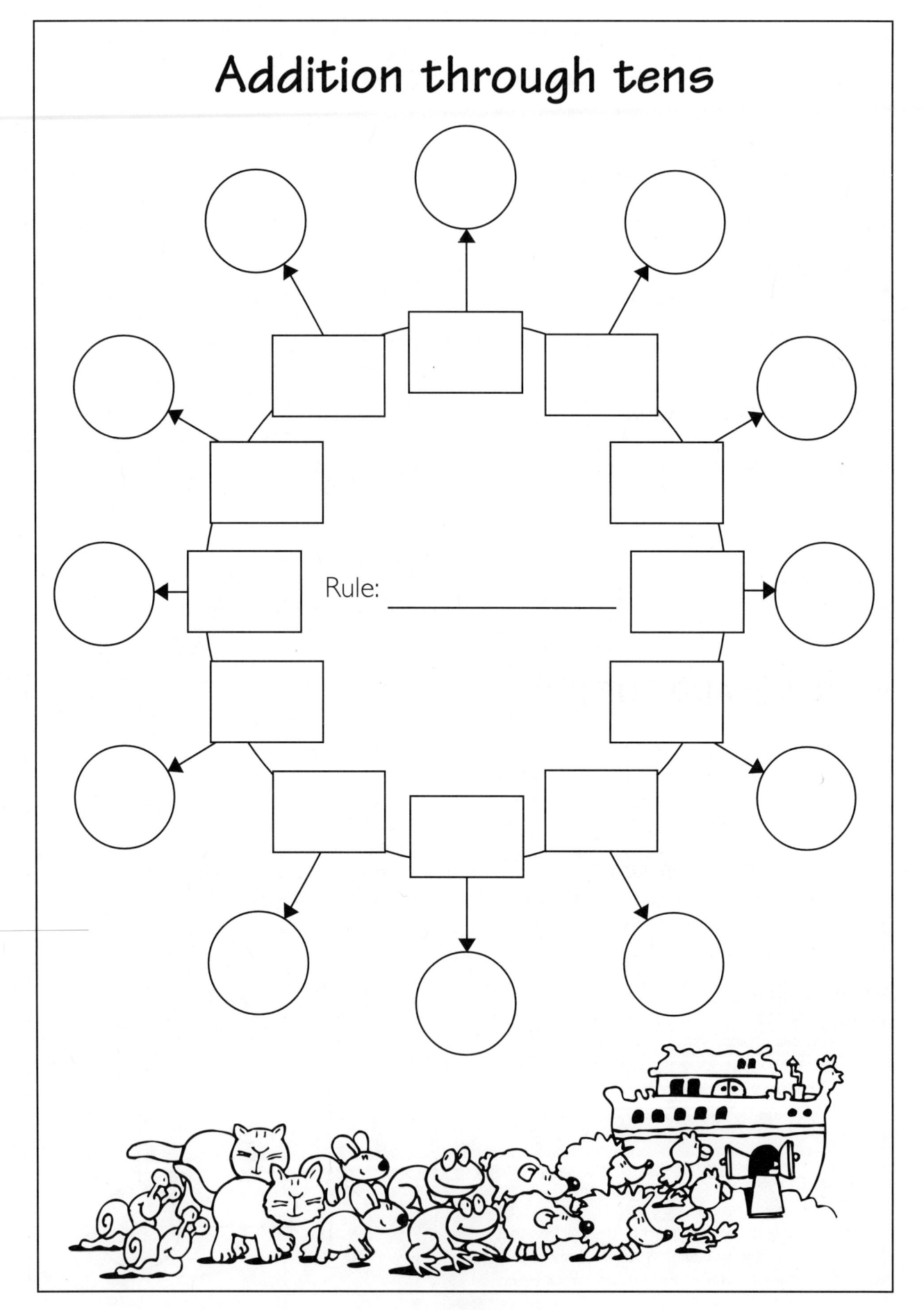

Addition through tens

Rule: _____

H, T AND U
ADDING TO TENS

Name _____   Date _____

Four in a line

A game for two players and a referee.

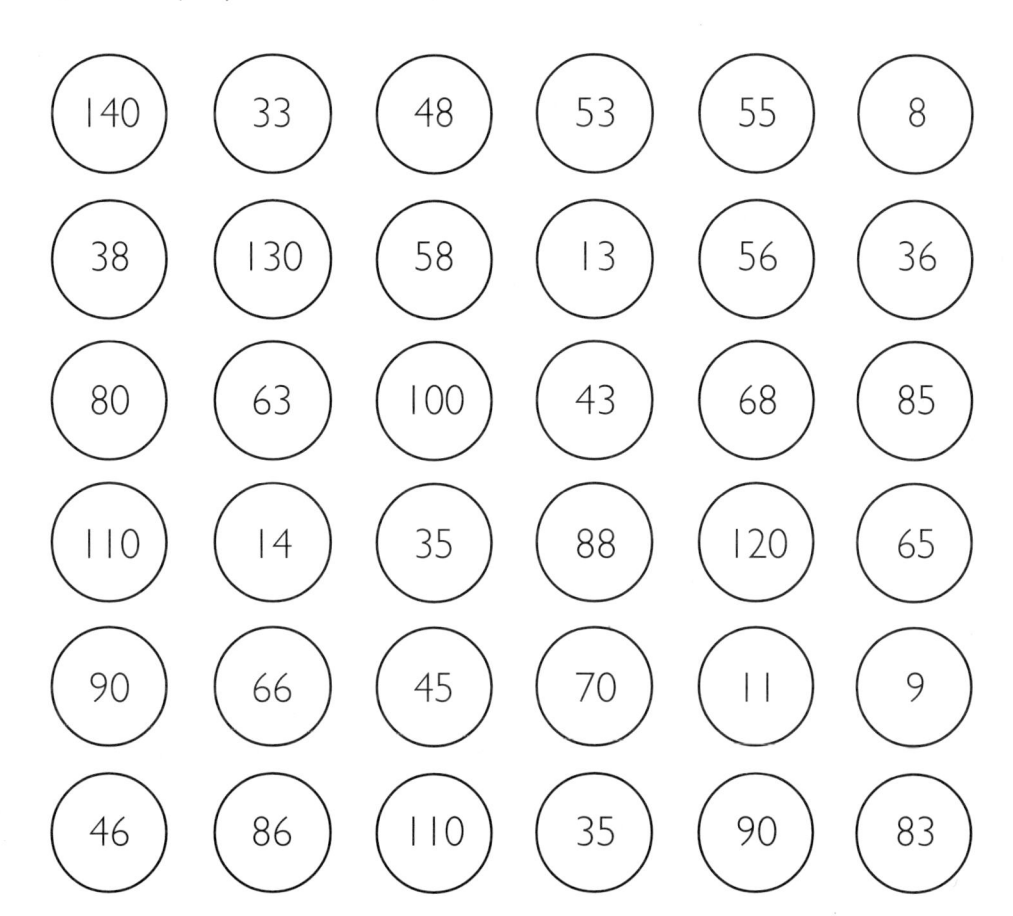

140	33	48	53	55	8
38	130	58	13	56	36
80	63	100	43	68	85
110	14	35	88	120	65
90	66	45	70	11	9
46	86	110	35	90	83

You will need: a different-coloured set of counters for each player; a calculator for the referee.

Rules
1 The players take turns to:
- choose any two of the numbers below;
- add them together to make a number on the grid above;
- cover the number on the grid with a counter.

2 The referee checks the players' sums with the calculator.

3 The first player to get four counters in a straight line in any direction is the winner.

| 3 | 5 | 6 | 8 | 30 | 40 | 50 | 60 | 80 |

H, T AND U
ADDING TO TENS

Name ——————————————   Date ——————————————

It all adds up

60	70	80	90	100
10	20	30	40	50
6	7	8	9	10
1	2	3	4	5

Rule:

Sums:

ADDITION AND SUBTRACTION

H, T AND U
ADDING TO TENS

Name _____ Date _____

It all adds up (2)

Rule:

H, T AND U
LOTS OF TENS

QUICK DOUBLES (2)

GROUP SIZE AND ORGANIZATION
Whole class (Y2/P3–Y3/P4).
DURATION
10–15 minutes.
LEARNING OBJECTIVE
To develop the skill of doubling 'tens' numbers mentally.

YOU WILL NEED
The hundreds, tens and units poster; a shuffled set of 'tens' number cards 10–100, a flip chart and marker pen (or chalkboard and chalk).

WHAT TO DO
Start by asking all the children to count aloud in 10s to 100. Can they count on to 200, 300 and so on?

Use the poster to talk about doubling numbers (adding two numbers that are the same). It will help if they have already done the activity 'Quick doubles' (page 12). Point to each 'tens' number in turn; ask individual children to give the doubled number and then to write the corresponding 'double sum' on the flip chart:
10 + 10 = 20
20 + 20 = 40 ... and so on.
Play the 'Quick doubles' game by holding up a 'tens' card and choosing a child to say the double number: 'Ian, double 20 is ...?' First play the game with the flip chart visible; then remove the flip chart and play again.

ASSESSMENT
Note whether the children can double the numbers mentally, or whether they need to look at the flip chart.

EXTENSION WORK
Play 'Quick trebles'. Invite the children to build up the pattern of 'treble sums' on the flip chart; then play the game as above.

IDEAS FOR DISPLAY
Charts showing patterns of double and treble numbers (represented as sums) can be displayed in the classroom as visual aids.

HUNT THE DOUBLE

GROUP SIZE AND ORGANIZATION
A group of 4 children, seated at a table or on the floor with the teacher (Y2/P3–Y3/P4).
DURATION
20–30 minutes.
LEARNING OBJECTIVE
To practise doubling 'tens' numbers.

YOU WILL NEED
Four sets of 'tens' cards 10–100, a flip chart and marker pen (or chalkboard and chalk).

WHAT TO DO
The pattern of 'double sums' from the previous activity should be displayed on the flip chart. Shuffle all the cards and spread them out face down on the table or floor. Play a game as described in 'Beat the teacher' (page 12): the children have to find two matching cards and say the total.

ASSESSMENT
Note whether the children can find the total mentally, or whether they need to look at the flip chart to find the answer.

H, T AND U
LOTS OF TENS

IDEAS FOR DIFFERENTIATION
Younger children could use four sets of cards showing only the 'tens' numbers 10–50.

Older children could play without the flip chart and use four sets of cards showing only the 'tens' numbers 50–100.

EXTENSION WORK
The children could play the 'Hunt the treble' game (see page 13), using three sets of 'tens' cards 10–100.

DOUBLES BINGO

GROUP SIZE AND ORGANIZATION
A group of 4 children, working with the teacher (Y2/P3–Y3/P4).
DURATION
20–30 minutes.
LEARNING OBJECTIVE
To distinguish between and become familiar with the doubles of 'ones' and 'tens' numbers.

YOU WILL NEED
A copy of photocopiable page 27, cut up and mounted on card to make four Bingo cards; a box of interlocking cubes or counters; a set of cards numbered 1–9 in units and a set numbered 10–100 in tens; a flip chart and marker pens (or chalkboard and chalk).

WHAT TO DO
Use the flip chart to display the pattern of 'double sums' in units and in tens. Give each child a Bingo card and seven interlocking cubes or counters. Explain that you are going to hold up a card showing either a 'ones' number or a 'tens' number, and you will say (for example) 'Double 4 needed'. The players have to work out the double number; if they have that number on their card, they should point to it.

Check each time that the child is pointing to the correct number; if so, he or she can put a cube or counter on the number. The first player to cover all of his or her numbers with cubes calls out 'Bingo!' Tell the children that they can look at the flip chart if they need help. Play the game a few times with the chart displayed; then remove it from view and play again.

ASSESSMENT
Check whether the children can recall the double numbers or work them out mentally, or whether they need to look at the chart.

IDEAS FOR DIFFERENTIATION
Try to make sure that the group playing the game are fairly matched in terms of ability. For less able children, the pace of the game may need to be a lot slower; help could be given initially by pointing to the corresponding 'double sum' on the chart and asking the group to say it together aloud before they look at their cards.

CIRCLE OF DOUBLES

GROUP SIZE AND ORGANIZATION
A group of 4 children working with the teacher (Y2/P3–Y3/P4).
DURATION
15–20 minutes.
LEARNING OBJECTIVE
To practise finding doubles of numbers.

YOU WILL NEED
A flip chart and marker pen (or chalkboard and chalk). For each child: two or more copies of photocopiable page 20, a pencil, a set of shuffled cards numbered 5–60 in 5s, a small margarine tub or box. Provide some Cuisenaire rods for any children who need help.

WHAT TO DO
Draw a large copy of the circle diagram from page 20 on the flip chart and write the numbers 5–60 in 5s in the boxes around the circle. (See 'Adding through tens' on page 17.) Give the children a copy each of photocopiable page 20. Ask them to write the numbers counting in 5s around the circle, using the flip chart to help them. When they have finished, ask them to write the rule 'Double the number' inside the circle.

ADDITION AND SUBTRACTION FACTS — RESOURCE BANK

H, T AND U
LOTS OF TENS

Give each child a shuffled set of numbered cards, in a pile face down in front of them, and a tub. Tell them that they have to take a card from the pile, double the number and write the answer in the correct circle on the sheet. They should then put the card in the tub and take another. The first player to use all his or her cards is the winner.

If there is time, give the children another copy of the sheet. Let them write the '5s' numbers in the boxes while you reshuffle the sets of numbered cards; then play the game again.

ASSESSMENT
Note which numbers the children are able to add mentally, and which numbers they double using rods, cubes or their fingers.

IDEAS FOR DIFFERENTIATION
For younger children, prepare some copies of the sheet with the numbers counting in 5s around the circle written in. Ask them to complete the sheet by doubling each of the numbers in order around the circle, so that they can establish the pattern.

For older children, prepare some copies of the sheet with random numbers between 15 and 49 (as in Figure 15) written around the circle. Ask them to record the double numbers.

EXTENSION WORK
A range of different activity sheets can be made from photocopiable page 20 by filling in the boxes with different numbers. These can be used as practice sheets for addition, subtraction, doubling, trebling, multiplying or halving numbers, depending on which 'rule' is given. The numbers used can be set according to the children's level of development. However, take care when including numbers lower than 10 for subtraction, as this may lead to the use of negative numbers.

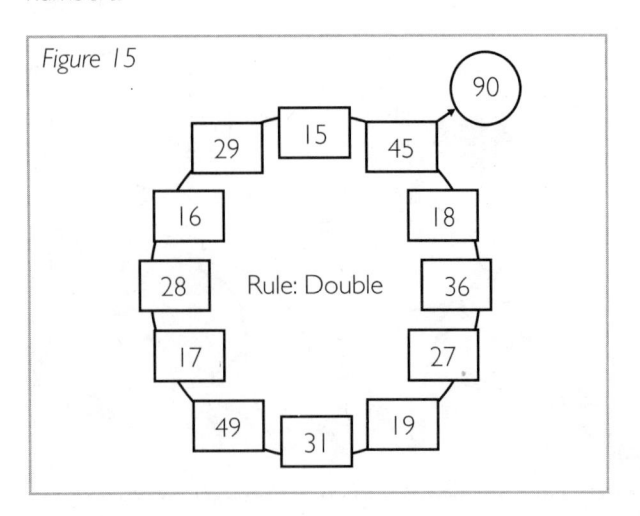

Figure 15

MAKING 100

GROUP SIZE AND ORGANIZATION
Children working individually in small groups (Y2/P3–Y3/P4).
DURATION
20–30 minutes.
LEARNING OBJECTIVE
To find different ways of making 100 by adding three 'tens' numbers.

YOU WILL NEED
A set of cards numbered 10–90 in 10s, plain or squared paper, pencils, a flip chart and marker pen (or chalkboard and chalk). Provide Cuisenaire rods or Dienes 'ten' rods for any child who needs help.

WHAT TO DO
Place the cards in a line, face up on the table. Tell the children that they have to look at the cards and think of different ways to make 100 by adding three 'tens' numbers, then write their answers as sums on paper. Demonstrate how the sums should be recorded on the flip chart – for example, 20 + 30 + 50 = 100. Ask them to find as many different sums as possible.

ASSESSMENT
Note whether the children can carry out the additions mentally or if they need to use structural apparatus.

IDEAS FOR DIFFERENTIATION
Younger or less able children could be given sets of ten '10' rods. Ask them to count out the rods aloud, in tens, to make sure they understand that the rods represent 100 split into 10s. Now ask them to divide the rods into three groups, count the rods in each group (in tens) and write the numbers on paper as an addition sum with a total of 100. (Demonstrate the recording on the flip chart.) Ask: *Can you find other ways to group the rods?* Tell the children that they must write down a sum for each way of grouping the rods.

EXTENSION WORK
If the children have solved the 'Magic square puzzle' (see page 14) successfully, they can be asked to work (individually or in pairs) on making a magic square with three 10s, three 20s and three 30s. Can they find the magic number? They could use squared paper to try out their ideas, and record the solution on a copy of photocopiable page 15. They could go on to try with three 20s, three 30s and three 40s (and so on).

H, T AND U
LOTS OF TENS

10							
							200
	18		180	8		80	
		60			16		160
	4		140	4			
		12				20	

		100			20		
	18			8		80	
	6		160				140
		40			14		
2			120	2			120

ADDITION AND SUBTRACTION

H, T AND U
TENS AND HUNDREDS

100 ADD TENS

GROUP SIZE AND ORGANIZATION
Whole class (Y2/P3–Y3/P4).
DURATION
15–20 minutes.
LEARNING OBJECTIVE
To recognize the place-value position of 'tens' in numbers above 100. To carry out addition in tens with numbers above 100, recording the totals correctly.

YOU WILL NEED
The hundreds, tens and units poster; a flip chart and marker pen (or chalkboard and chalk); a set of 'tens' number cards (10–100).

WHAT TO DO
Draw a large diagram on the flip chart of a HTU bead abacus showing a representation of 100 (see Figure 16). Leave enough space underneath to record sums for the addition of tens up to 190 (see below).

Ask the children to count aloud to 1000, first in hundreds and then in tens. Point to each 'hundreds' number on the poster as the children reach it.

Use the bead abacus diagram to explain how one hundred is represented in numerals (1 hundred, 0 tens and 0 units). Add 10 to the abacus by drawing one bead on the 'tens' stick; pointing to the abacus 'sticks', say 'One hundred and one ten and no units.' Write the sum '100 + 10 = 110' underneath, and ask the children to read the sum aloud together.

Draw another 'ten' bead on the abacus, point at each 'stick' and ask the children: *How many hundreds? Tens? Units?* Write the appropriate sum underneath the first sum, and ask the children to read it aloud. Invite a child to draw another bead on the abacus, write the sum underneath and say it aloud. Continue until nine beads have been drawn on the tens 'stick'.

Remove these 'workings' from sight and play the '100 add tens' game. Shuffle a set of 'tens cards' and hold up a card. Ask a child to add that number to 100 and write the answer on the flip chart. Ask the rest of the class to verify the child's answer, then clean the flip chart and repeat.

ASSESSMENT
Note whether the children can add a 'tens' number to 100 and write out the sum accurately.

EXTENSION WORK
Start with 200 displayed on the bead abacus, and build up the pattern of adding tens. Then start with 300, and so on.

When the children are familiar with the pattern of adding tens up to 990, play a more challenging version of the game by using a shuffled set of 'hundreds' cards (100–900) and a shuffled set of 'tens' cards (10–90) in two separate piles. Hold up a card from each pile; ask a child to add the numbers together and write the answer on the board.

This game could be made into a small-group (or individual) activity for further practice. Each child is given a piece of paper, a pencil and shuffled sets of 'hundreds' and 'tens' cards placed face down in separate piles. The children should take one card from each pile and record the sum each time. Allow them to draw a bead abacus if they are unsure.

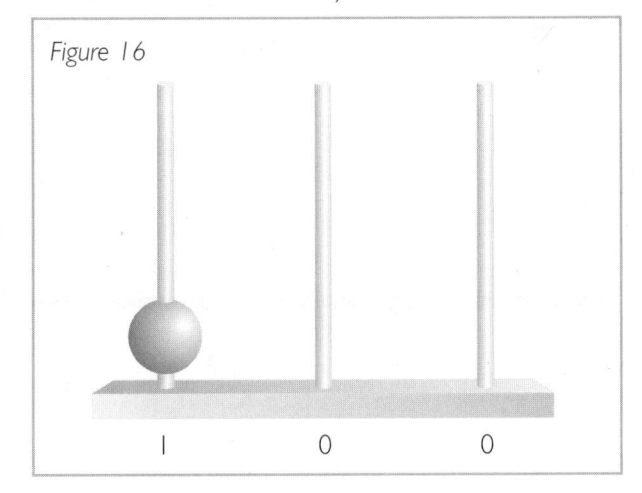

Figure 16

GROW A 200 PLANT

GROUP SIZE AND ORGANIZATION
A group of 4–6 children (Y2/P3–Y3/P4).
DURATION
20–30 minutes.
LEARNING OBJECTIVE
To find different ways of making 200 by adding six 'tens' numbers.

YOU WILL NEED
Photocopiable page 30, pencils, one set per child of cards numbered in tens (10–90), crayons or felt-tipped pens.

WHAT TO DO
Lay all the 'tens' cards face up on the table, and give each child a copy of photocopiable page 30. Tell the

H, T AND U
TENS AND HUNDREDS

children that they have to use six 'tens' cards to make 200. When they have decided what numbers they need, they should write each number on a leaf of the plant. Encourage them to consider strategies such as:
◆ finding two different ways to make 100 with three 'tens' cards;
◆ using double or treble numbers.
When they have written in the numbers, they should write '**200 plant**' in the space on the plant pot. They can then draw a flower at the top, colour the leaves and decorate the pot. They can go on to make another 200 plant using a different set of numbers.

ASSESSMENT
Note whether the children are able to make 200 with six 'tens' numbers by working mentally, or whether they need to use rods or fingers.

IDEAS FOR DIFFERENTIATION
Younger children could make a 20 plant, using sets of cards numbered in units to 10. If children need help, provide Cuisenaire rods or Dienes 'tens' rods for them to match to the numbers on the cards.

Older children could use the sheet with sets of cards numbered in hundreds and tens to make, for example, a 450 plant with six numbers. They could use the space at the top of the sheet to add more leaves.

IDEAS FOR DISPLAY
The completed plants can be mounted for display. Use strips of paper to make a border: the children can paint wavy stems with leaves on each strip, and stick circular tissue-paper flowers along the stems.

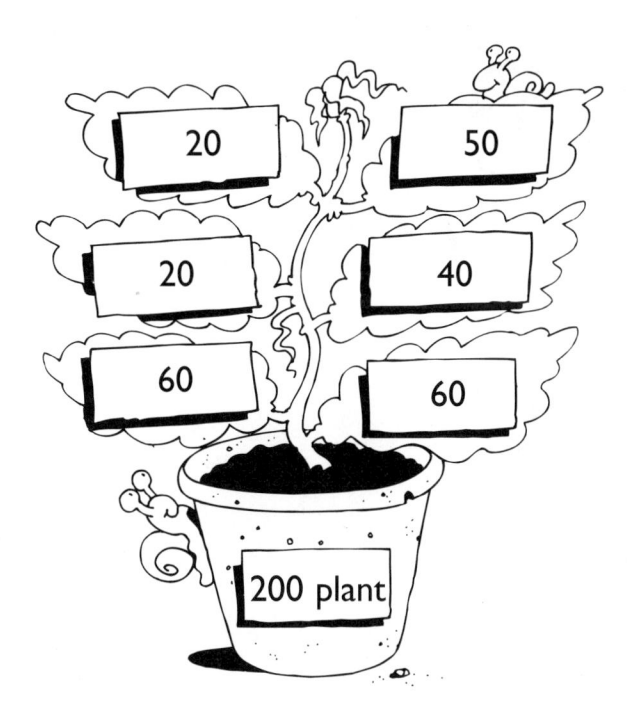

OFF THE BOARD

GROUP SIZE AND ORGANIZATION
A board game for 4 players, with teacher supervision (Y2/P3–Y3/P4).
DURATION
20–30 minutes.
LEARNING OBJECTIVE
To subtract multiples of 10 through hundreds from 500.

YOU WILL NEED
Four copies of photocopiable page 31, mounted on card and laminated; an enlarged (A3) copy or OHT of page 31; four sets of cards numbered 10–60 in 10s; four coloured counters or cubes.

WHAT TO DO
Display the enlarged copy of photocopiable page 31; ask the children to count back in tens aloud together, while you point to each number in turn. Shuffle all the cards together and place them face down in a pile on the table.

Give each player a board and a coloured counter or cube. Tell the children that they must start with their counter on the 500 square. The players take turns to take a card from the pile. They must subtract the 'tens' number from 500 and move their counter to the new number square, then place their card on a 'discard' pile. The first player to reach 0 and get 'off the board' wins. The winner must have picked up a card that moves the counter into the 0 box, with nothing left over; if the card picked takes the player below zero, the counter does not move and play passes to the next player.

ASSESSMENT
Note whether the children can carry out a subtraction mentally and move their counter directly to the new number, or whether they need to count back to the number in tens and move one square at a time.

IDEAS FOR DIFFERENTIATION
For younger children, make copies of the board using the numbers 50–0 in units. Play with four sets of cards numbered 1–6 (shuffled together).

For older children, make the game more challenging by introducing a dice marked with three + and three – signs. The children have to throw a dice each time they take a card, then move either backwards or forwards according to the throw. (If they throw a + at the start of the game, they cannot move.)

ADDITION AND SUBTRACTION FACTS

H, T AND U
TENS AND HUNDREDS

Name _____   Date _____

Grow a number plant

H, T AND U
TENS AND HUNDREDS

500	400	300	200	100
490	390	290	190	90
480	380	280	180	80
470	370	270	170	70
460	360	260	160	60
450	350	250	150	50
440	340	240	140	40
430	330	230	130	30
420	320	220	120	20
410	310	210	110	10

0

ADDITION AND SUBTRACTION

PHOTOCOPIABLE RESOURCE BANK

H, T AND U
DOUBLING HUNDREDS

DOUBLE TALK

GROUP SIZE AND ORGANIZATION
Whole class (Y2/P3–Y3/P4).
DURATION
15–20 minutes.
LEARNING OBJECTIVE
To build the pattern of 'double hundred' sums, finding the totals, with numbers 100–1000.

YOU WILL NEED
The hundreds, tens and units poster; a flip chart and marker pen (or chalkboard and chalk).

WHAT TO DO
Ask all the children to count aloud in hundreds to 2000. Do this a few times, as they may require some prompting to count through 1000 at first.

Write the first 'double sum' on the flip chart (100 + 100 =) and invite a child to say the doubled number and write the answer on the board. Repeat the process for the second 'double sum'. Invite another child to write the third sum on the board with the answer. Continue up to double 1000.

Now point to different hundreds numbers on the poster, asking a child to double the number and say the answer each time. Tell the children that they can look at the flip chart if they need help. When they appear confident, remove the chart from view and continue.

ASSESSMENT
Note whether the children can double the numbers mentally, or whether they need to use the flip chart.

EXTENSION WORK
Point to any number (hundreds, tens or units) on the poster, asking the children to find the double.

Play the game 'Beat the teacher' (see page 12) using four sets of 'hundreds' cards (100–1000).

Play the game 'Hunt the treble' (see page 13) using three sets of 'hundreds' cards (100–1000).

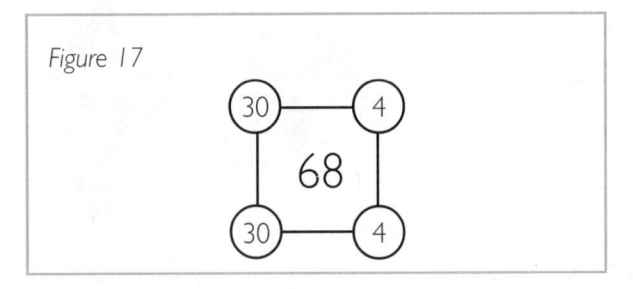

Figure 17

30 — 4
  68
30 — 4

MIXED DOUBLES

GROUP SIZE AND ORGANIZATION
Group of 4–6 children (Y3/P4).
DURATION
20–30 minutes.
LEARNING OBJECTIVE
To practise adding together two different doubled numbers in hundreds, tens or units.

YOU WILL NEED
A flip chart and marker pen (or chalkboard and chalk), photocopiable page 23, pencils, calculators, three sets of nine cards numbered 1–9, 10–90 and 100–1000.

WHAT TO DO
Use the flip chart to build up the pattern of doubles in units, tens and hundreds. Ask what the next 'sum' will be each time, and invite a child to say the answer.

Mix all the cards together and shuffle them. Give each child a copy of photocopiable page 23. Tell the children that you will deal them two cards each. They must write the numbers in the top circles on the first diagram on the sheet, and again in the lower circles; then they must add them all together and write the total in the middle of the diagram. Draw an example on the flip chart (see Figure 17). When they have done this, they give back the cards and receive two more.

Encourage the children to consider the strategy of finding each of the doubles first before working out the total. Tell them that they can use the flip chart and write 'workings' on the sheet to help them. If they get stuck, they can use a calculator; if they do so, ask them to draw a circle around the diagram on the sheet. To make this activity a game, declare that when all the sheets are finished, the one with the fewest circles around the diagrams wins. If no child has drawn circles, the first child to finish with all answers correct wins.

ASSESSMENT
Note whether the children can add the numbers together correctly using mental arithmetic, whether they need to consult the flip chart and/or write down 'workings', or whether they need to use a calculator.

IDEAS FOR DIFFERENTIATION
For younger children, use only sets of cards numbered 1–5, 10–50 and 100–500. For less able children, use only sets of cards numbered 1–5 and 10–50. For older children, use sets of cards numbered 5–9, 50–90 and 500–900. Remove the flip chart from view.